Who'll Pick the Morning Rose?

Who'll Pick the Morning Rose?

A Book of Poetry
by Mary Heyborne

WHO'LL PICK THE MORNING ROSE?
A Book of Poetry by Mary Heyborne

Published by Mary Heyborne, Sedona, Arizona

Printed in the United States
Book design: Jane Perini, ThunderMountainDesign.com

ISBN: 978-0-9779260-2-2

Acknowledgments

Some of these poems have appeared in:

Bride's Magazine
Sedona Magazine
"The Coming of Dawn" (anthology)
Sandcutters—Journal of the Arizona
State Poetry Society

~ ~ ~ ~ ~

~~~~~

"Who'll Pick the Morning Rose?"
is the author's affirmation
that life and poetry—
as well as their gifts of love, truth, and beauty—
are expanded when shared.

Her contemplations are influenced by roles
as wife, mother, and professional potter,
but she writes for everyman
in her celebration of the commonplace
and her quest for universal truths.

~~~~~

For Leck

Contents

~ Art and Nature ~

~ Time and Place ~

~ Post Diagnosis ~

Introduction

R aise a child, plant a tree, and write a poem. This purported recipe for a full life was extolled to me as a young girl and struck a chord in my romantic nature that continues to reverberate. For this reason I found it difficult to accept my husband's coolness toward the recipe when I shared it with him, even though his technical background and my artistic bent often caused us to see things differently.

"Remember—children, trees, and poems," I frequently teased. No discussion was needed about the first part—we both wanted children, and they came to us quite naturally. But trees and poems were another matter.

On our first Mother's Day in a new home, Leck got out of bed unusually early—before our young boys were awake. We never got up on weekends before the kids forced it! But, deciding he must be going to make a special Mother's Day breakfast for me, I rolled over and snuggled back into the covers.

Later, I did arise to a gourmet omelet, but my real surprise came when Leck drew back the drapes in the breakfast area to reveal a newly planted apple tree.

"You write the poem," he bargained with a smile, recalling the recipe.

"What a beautiful gift," I exclaimed, "but I think the recipe means we both need to tree and poem. We both want full lives," I needled.

"I think that I shall never see/A poem lovely as a tree," he countered in staccato tones that would have made Kilmer wince.

"Doesn't count," I said. "I'll help you write a poem, and you can help me plant our next tree."

I liked to write poems, but when I shared them with him he was uncomfortable with the emotion and intimacy. I came to realize he would never write a poem himself and quit mentioning the recipe. I found myself writing less, as well, but did go on to plant a few trees.

Meanwhile, Leck became more consumed by his career. What time he could claim for himself he devoted to gardening, and through the years I watched with pleasure as his roses flourished and his vegetable and herb gardens became more exotic and fruitful.

When Leck retired I went back to college and steeped myself in poetry. I almost swooned when my handsome English Literature professor recited Keats and Donne but continued to find no encouragement when I ventured to read aloud at home. I did begin writing poetry again, however, and one morning when Leck got out of bed I rolled into the warm spot he left and, without thinking, recited a poem I had written for one of my classes:

When he leaves our bed before me
I roll into the newly vacant space
Delicious with his warmth and scent
> *And savor every trace*
> *Of the night just spent.*

He reached down and hugged me, and I could see my poem had touched him.

I dressed leisurely then followed him downstairs to the kitchen. My eyes were immediately drawn to the breakfast table, and they filled with tears as I approached.

Through all these years he had remembered our recipe.

Angled across a fresh sheet of parchment lay a perfect long-stemmed pink rose. A poem from his garden.

~ ~ ~ ~ ~

Loveds

WHO'LL PICK THE MORNING ROSE?

Which one of us will bolt awake
And reach in vain across the bed
Then rail against the mounting ache?
Which one will face the daily dread
Of going on alone?

Who'll make the bed once made by two
And close the house against the rain?
Which one will choose the morning brew,
And grind the beans, and feel the pain
Of making half a pot?

Who'll face the morning news alone
At angles to an empty chair?
Who'll lift the ringing telephone
For family news — and ache to share?
Who'll pick the morning rose?

I'M GLAD YOU KNEW ME THEN

Trembling
from white dress
to undress white
seeing by moonlight
myself
reflected in your eyes
watching you
absorb my nakedness
first time seen
sweet eighteen.

Your burning gaze
seared my image
on your sight
to last
undimmed by tears
or years
and when you see me now
imposes yet
my youth
upon your eye.

WHEN HE LEAVES OUR BED BEFORE ME

When he leaves our bed before me
I roll into the newly-vacant space,
Delicious with his warmth
And scent,
And savor every trace
Of the night just spent.

TOGETHER

Time was we spun in separate orbs
Attracted through a universe between —
A vast and non-conductive space
Permitting only mild libration
And then a firmer oscillation
Toward together.

Oh, yes! that first together
When non-conductors were removed
And magnetism pulled us into one —
A primal clash
Then such delicious spinning
Before the hurling back
To separate orbs.

And now, in frightening dependence
Born of a new together,
We listen for the other's breath,
Touch more, cling tighter — longer,
Bracing for the last together
And the breach of our forever
When our mass is halved again.

REMEMBER WE WERE YOUNG

When frailties overtake us
and our steps are stiff and slow,
remember how we ran—
your father on the basketball court,
the track, the football field,
or across the fields he helped to farm
and I down hot dry streets
with wind in my corn-silk hair.

When our skin is blotched and wrinkled
and our hair is thin and white,
and a film has stretched across our eyes,
remember we were beautiful
and very much admired.

When we seem unsure or frightened
and our confidence has gone,
remember the courage we brought to life,
how we dared to stretch,
unwilling to play it safe.

When one is gone and one remains
with welled-up eyes
and aching, empty arms,
remember the love that made you—
remember we were young.

MORNING RITUAL

You leave our bed in the early morning chill.
I hear your barefoot steps fade down the hall.
The scroll from China rustles as you pass.
The furnace moans—you've reached the heat control.
Water runs in the back-hall bath.

I halt my breath for sounds of your return—
The scroll, then footsteps that retrace your walk.
Your body curls around my fetal pose—
Two well-worn puzzle pieces interlock
And cling in comfort, sharing warm.

GIFT OF LOVE
(for my mother)

For giving me courage to meet life head on
And freedom to chart my own path cross the sun —
For enduring with patience my muddling through
And saying, "Explore, I'll be waiting for you" —
For giving me roots and giving me wings —
  Accept my gift of love.

For pointing out joys in each day that went by —
For respecting the times when I needed to cry,
Knowing whether to help me or let me alone —
For sharing your thoughts though I guarded my own —
For living each day and then moving on —
  Accept my gift of love.

For showing me faith and teaching me prayer,
Acknowledging beauty and good everywhere —
For commending music, drama, and books —
For saying "you can" with encouraging looks
Then praising my efforts, successful or not —
  Accept my gift of love.

For birthday cakes baked before it was light
And for Christmas dresses sewn late at night —
Whether braiding the Maypole, trimming the tree,
Making Christmas candles or candies with me —
For making holidays memorable times —
  Accept my gift of love.

For secrets you shared and secrets you kept—
For the laughs you laughed and the tears you wept—
For showing me steadfastness lived to the end,
The importance of work, the value of friends—
For examples of honesty, fairness, and truth—
   Accept my gift of love.

I cling to my husband in tear-flooded joy,
My heart nearly bursting with love for my boys—
Then I think of the times you've held me near
And know for a lifetime you've held me dear.
For being the one who taught me to love—
   Accept my gift of love.

OF DRAGON CAVES AND UNICORNS

Now that you're grown, my grandson,
Do you recall your baby years
When your dimpled hand
Reached out for me
To explore some secret place?

Soft but strong
Your hand
Was always sure of where to lead,
Each time farther than before —
To the ant hills
Then the dragon caves —
Your open heart endowing me
With sweet philosophy.

Oh, how I hope
That you
As I
Still believe in unicorns!

FINGERPRINTS

Each child
stirs different feelings
within a mother's heart
affecting warmth
and cadence,
stoking higher heat
or quicker beat
that lingers longer,
echoes stronger,
and moves the heart
to elevate
excite, expand, endure.

Each child
leaves different fingerprints
upon a mother's heart.

VIGIL

This used to be my father—
This heaving, sheet-draped form
With lidded eyes, spectral set
In an unfamiliar face.
Now all that's left
Are labored breaths
And little time, I'm told—
But whatever time he had for me
He gave up long ago.

With his trucker's job
I wasn't sure
Just when he left for good,
But we were young—
We four and Mom—
When he went off to work one day
"And . . just . . kept . . going,"
I overheard
A neighbor lady say.

My tears were mostly for my mom
But my older brother, too.
He was so much his father's son—
I feared he suffered more than I
Left fatherless with no good-bye,
And, yes, I cried for him.
But I never talked about my dad
To him—
Or anyone.

I count the breaths, each rise and fall.
I miss my babes at home.
It seems much more than yesterday
Our early morning still
Was shattered
By that piercing ring
And then my uncle's mournful voice
Across a hundred wintry miles
Conveyed the solemn news.

My tears were for my uncle then —
That steadfast patriarch,
Cruelly tempered
At deathbed scenes
With parents,
Siblings,
Child.
He shall not be lone witness here
To the winnowing of beloveds.

Below the distent stomach hump
A circle looms and spreads —
Transparent, widening to reveal
His lifeless source of life.
My source — my life,
Affirms my brain.
Atop the form a folded sheet is lain
And then unfurled,
The wet one drawn away.

My weary uncle leaves the room,
And I approach the bed.
I know we shared some happy times —
Why, suddenly, instead,
Do I recall a day at school
And a registration form —
How I trembled filling in a word,
Unacknowledged
Up till then?

"Divorced."
That word—ubiquitous today—
Was whispered then in Utah towns,
If said at all,
Like "cancer"—and "death."
That word—when written down—
Was chiseled in my brain
And, like some cruel epiphany,
Marked my childhood's end.

The smell of liquor lessens
In the breaths that rack him now.
Spasms grip
His ghostly form and face.
I search for recognition
In the flutterings of his eyes.
"Can he know I'm here?"
I ask a nurse.
"Probably," she lies.

I do not hear my uncle's step
Nor feel my husband's touch.
I'm rapt—
In the womb of childhood lost—
Secure in Daddy's love.
My transport ends as a doctor's words
Abort me from those years—
Expel me once again too soon—
"He's gone." So, too, my tears.

ON THE PASSING OF FRIENDS

When friends flourished around us
As in a forest stand —
Some in reach
And others farther out
We simply knew were there —
We lived secure.

Now, one by one,
The sentinels fall
Leaving gaps along the ridge
Where storms sweep down
And buffet us —
And we wilt for want of shade.

HER DAUGHTER—NOT HER NURSE

I want to be her daughter
not her nurse,
she said.
Let others check her vitals,
tend her fevers,
give the meds.
I want to hold
her trembling hands,
look deep into her eyes,
recall the good times,
restate my love,
embrace our last goodbyes.

Cruelly—or blessedly—
the days were few,
but there was sweet exchange
as mother braced
to leave her child
and the daughter to remain.
The circle closes once again—
smaller than before—
as arms enfolding,
tightening,
round the daughter
as she mourns.

REMEMBRANCE

Our world is smaller,
contracted from yesterday
when our curious
and well-traveled
friend
shared this sphere —

from a distance, yes,
but still was here
in calls — and clippings —
reminding us of common pasts
and friends
and glory days.

Our world is smaller
but the loosened skin
on this contracted sphere
drapes us in comfort
and sweet remembrance
that he was here.

On Being and Becoming

PRAYER TO THE MUSE

O, Muse,
Fair daughter of Mnemosyne,
Run barefoot through my brain.
Teach me to prize the commonplace
As part of the divine.
Companion me on morning walks
Amid the shrines of Pan.
Unscale my eyes to color, light —
Attune my ears to song.

Should discords of the day distract
And thwart the poet's will
Desert me not, Amorphous One —
Be succor to me still.
Sit lotus-legged on my desk —
Infuse, instill, inspire!
Embolden me to lift my pen,
Erato . . . Erato . . .
Erato!

UNCENTERED

I don't feel caught in a widening gyre
turning
whirling
hurling apart.
Rather
imperceptibly slowed
I spin
out of grace
uncentered.

THE SLIPPING AWAY

The slipping away was gradual —
spanning years —
the stifling of emotion barely noticed.
The heaviness of spirit at nightfall
balanced morning's leaden heart.

Time,
no longer valued,
passed unheeded
but still its threads were woven —
lacing dullness and acquiescence
through the once-vivid fabric of my life.
Distorted patterns emerged —
uncreative,
carelessly woven,
alternating rows of tension
and ennui,
then flat,
colorless.

The heaviness of spirit at nightfall
balanced morning's leaden heart.

SEEKING SECURITY

A child
learning to walk
grasps another's hand
or, absent that,
enfists a toy
as Dumbo held his feather.

The seeking
of security,
so natural in a child,
is spurned
in vital middle years
as casting off a tether

and then
again is natural
as aging lovers reach
to touch a shoulder,
brush a cheek —
secure beside the other —

and, even in sleep,
shun separateness
for the comfort of together —
two bodies, one body,
two bodies, one body,
. . . one body.

RENEWAL

With limbs flung wide
I lie in hunger on my meadow floor
an empty vessel
drained by life's routines
renew
restore

I feel at once a part of earth
a part of sky
sink heavily into the ground
and yet I fly
into that ceiling filled with sun
from earthbound shade

An overwhelming silence
fills my ears
then interludes of birdsong
rustling leaves
and whir of insect wings
symphonic
mute

My nostrils capture
intermingling scents
of soil and leaf
and bloom
I taste them all
subtle
intense

Drops of rain
and dew
and tear
mix trickles in the crackling grass
dry
damp

I kiss the wind
her sweet and intermittent breath
now cool
now warm

the sun seduces me

I am

BREATHING DEEP

What makes me cling
So hungrily
To life and afterlife,
Concern myself
With evermores—
Breathe shallow?

Immortal words,
Eternal clay
Encroach upon my hours.
I fill my kiln
And fill the page—
Breathe shallow.

I mean to speak
Unhurried words,
Take time for smiles that linger,
Reach out and touch
Another's hand—
Breathe deep.

I want to roam
The realms of Pan
Companioned by an earnest child
And join a friend
Across a cup—
Breathe deep.

Let me live on
In syllables
And vessels vitrified
But, also, in
The child—and friend—
Breathing deep.

THE COOL SIDE OF MY PILLOW

On fitful late night wanderings
Through every shade of dark
I cry for succor from my muse —
A literary spark
To conjure up elusive words
Or bridge a remnant thought,
An antidote for sleeplessness
That roils, success or not.

Footfalls whisper through the house —
Each surface echoes gloom
As, tile to rug, this passing shade
Trails longings room to room
Then turns — returns — when dawn exhales
Her rosy, soft alarms
To the cool side of my pillow
And the warm side of your arms.

Art and Nature

ON THE IMMORTALITY OF JOHN KEATS

Meteorlike, Keats streaked across
Our literary sky—
A burst of brilliance, trailing rhyme,
Hailed forever in poesy's shrine.
In manhood's bloom his fire was quenched
By Death,
And yet he lives
In the eternal incandescence of his odes.

I do not know
If some museum shelf
Guards yet his celebrated urn
Behind locked glass
With uniformed attendant standing by,
But, oh, I know
How sharp its image is aburn
Upon my brain
And how the memory in my fingertips retains
Each subtle tracing of relief—
Exquisite rise and fall—
Carved in that venerated vessel of his ode.

At pleasure I revive his sylvan scene
With lovers poised apant beneath the trees
Forever breathless in their bliss
Anticipating—
They and I—
A perfect consummation, yes,
But more than this—
Truth unchanging in a world of change.

HAIKU

Winter, wearing white,
Drags her cloak across the field
Erasing autumn.

IN SEARCH OF HALE-BOPP

I looked too early
And looked too hard
With chin set firm —
Binoculars aready —
Puffing my way to higher ground,
Cursing any cloud that cluttered
And in frustration finally muttered,
"Forget it, Hale-Bopp!"

Another night
I stepped outside
To breathe the new spring air
And turned unthinking to the sky
With naked heart and naked eye
And there she was —
Bold and bright —
Doing comet things.

I watched her other nights —
Not staring overlong,
Infringing on her piece of sky,
But honoring her place in time
And feeling she respected mine —
A sweet exchange
Between two spheres
Then she was gone.

Now when I think of Hale-Bopp
I do not mourn her loss
But celebrate the nights we touched —
Travelers of earth and space
Acknowledging the other's place —
And bold and bright
She streaks again
Across my naked heart.

SPRING

At the window
I am stunned.
It seems that overnight
The earth relaxed
And let the stalks push through,
Erect and tall
Supporting crowns
To flaunt across the sky,
Shouting spring
In colors that explode my heart.

POTTER AND POT

The living clay
Breathes strongly in my hands
In rhythm with my body as I wedge.
The clay exhales
Neath the heel of my palm
And breathes in as the spiral is raised.

I learned as a child
The seduction of clay—
It oozed through my naked toes
When in sensual abandon
I danced in the rain
Yielding to the wet earth's embrace.

Now I round the living earth
And listen as I thump
To voices deep in the clay—
To murmurs and music
Spanning the years
From the Anasazi's day.

Then I move the rounded form
To our tryst on the wheel
Where, as partners impelled to create,
We surrender ourselves
To centrifugal force—
Each seeking that centered state.

A crescendo is stoked
In the heart of the clay
In our foreplay of whisper and touch
And erupts when the center
Is entered and drawn
Out and up in a joyous thrust.

Ah! I am not Keats
Nor you a Grecian urn,
But your beauty and truth must live on.
Child of the earth,
Born of my touch,
Taste the fire—feel eternity's bond!

Your import to history
Will ever be hailed
While none shall remember my name,
And after I'm covered
With flesh of your flesh
You'll tempt others to dance in the rain.

RITUAL IN THE DESERT

A supernatural stillness rules the desert
In the early morning hours.
There is a purity—a clarity—
A celebrious thinness of the air
That lengthens my stride
As I bisect the flat landscape before me.
A raw clay pot is cradled in one arm,
And a bucket of water suspends from the other.
In another time or place
The bucket would be burdensome,
But just before dawn in the desert
It floats—in proud defiance of gravity.

When no vestige of civilization corrupts my view
I halt my linear trek
And kneel to prepare a ritual site.
I hollow out an earthen nest
To hold my earthen pot
Then place the uninitiated vessel—
Newly flowered, untouched by fire—
Into her crucible.
In that instant
The day's first flash of sun
Strikes me, like a prism,
And I reflect my joy.

Circling out in ever-widening orbs
I scour the desert floor
For twigs, and brush, and gifts of dung
Then eddy back to stack the pyre—
Not with the grief and foreboding
Of some ancient Abraham or Agamemnon
But joyfully, as the enabler
Of immortality for my maiden pot.
My moves scarce stir the morning air,
Nor do I wake the gods
When, with a flourish of Promethean power,
I light the fire.

For hours I feed the hungry beast
That licks around the pot
Then fall asleep when the sun is high —
When the sun is high and hot
And I am spent as the fire is spent.
The air is heavy now
And weighs me to the rock
That is my crucible.
Infused with light and heat, I dream
Until a raven's caw
Awakens me to check the coals —
Still glowing when the air is stirred.

Hypnotically, I watch the mound
Of ashes blow away
And choke with awe at the unveiling
Of the metamorphosed clay.
Then, trembling, I immerse my pot
In water, with a prayer.
Baptized, her beauty transcends my dream.
I raise her high — then higher!
My body sways — drawn into dance
That feeds my frenzied joy —
Til dizzied, breathless, I fall to earth
Clutching her like a poem.

TLAQUEPAQUE TULIPS

Throughout the courtyards tulips blaze
In gloried counterpoint.
Symphonic oranges and reds
Compete with yellows, pinks, and whites
In angel-wooing strains.

The Emperors bestride the scene—
Crescendos hail their march.
Their centers commandeer the sun
And hurtle back such light
To blind the eye.

Flamboyant blooms defying time
Swagger in their riot
Then tumble through the vivid now
To the past, pastel and quiet,
Trailing pianissimos.

STRAWBERRY

Strawberry—
warm with morning sun,
fat with flavor,
borne by lover's hand
as is my morning rose,
lifted to my lips
as for a kiss
and hungrily received,
rolled and savored by my tongue.

The ruddy flesh
resists the first advances of my teeth
then bursts
and floods—
strawberry.

OPEN HOUSE AT CURT WALTERS' STUDIO

All my senses stir, pulled off center
by paintings that reach out from walls
in the flicker of candlelight
and the wafting perfume of oils.
Echoes of Mussorgsky's "Pictures . . ."
rise from the morning crowd,
creating a restless counterpoint
of ambiguous scenes and sounds.

Cathedrals and canyons open wide,
draw me inside their sacred spheres,
encircle me with sheltering arms,
and breathe hymnals in my ears.
A paean, a prayer, a poem rise up—
inflating hearts with reverence
and too much beauty—exploding
awe and innocence.

Flowers in saturate, sultry hues
smolder on a cobalt bed—
ruby fruits and Bali bacchanals
exploit the palette's reds—
sensuous echoes of oboe and flute,
from paintings with pastel fire,
recall Debussy's successive scenes
of longings and desire.

The daughters of Mnemosyne—
loosed, dancing in the throng—
juxtapose the sister arts
in pulsing undersong.
Sensual feasting consumes the hours
without satiety.
Dizzied from waves of emotion,
I cling to "L'Après-Midi . . ."

MOONLIGHT THROUGH LACE

Moonlight,
Filtering through the pear tree just outside,
Shadows the curtains
With artistic flair —
Exploiting values on the lace,
Lights and darks —
Creating angels
With arms outstretched
That dance across the folds.

Oh, happy angels,
Blessed, I think, to have such grace
And bear with lightness
Your angelic charge!
But now
An intervening cloud deletes the scene —
This otherworldly Etch-a-Sketch,
In one bold stroke,
Is bare.

Time and Place

FROM RIM TO RIM

Today when I view the Grand Canyon
It will be through older eyes
And across the gorge from our honeymoon site
Of thirty years ago.
Dare I hope to bridge such time and space
And feel again the awe
That marked that earlier, magical time
When the colors of the North Rim
Blazed in the glow of newly consummated love?

As I near the first overlook
Tears—borne on a tide of anticipation—
Well and flow.
I step to the edge and reel,
Stunned by grandeur and hue.
A vacuum force from the canyon's core
Sucks a gasp from my strictured throat.
Still blurred,
My eyes move down the near face of the chasm—
Tracing each erosional form.
Dramatic escarpments and rippled plateaus
Recall my own
Upheavals and calms.
Labyrinthine valleys of darkness
Punctuated by pinnacles of light
Lead me on.
From the farthest point on the canyon floor
My eyes scale the other side—
Slowly, to its distant rim.
Could it be two innocent lovers
Still haunt that timeless realm?
Where had they stood? And, at eternity's bid,
Had they looked across for us?

A familiar hand takes hold of mine.
I turn my eyes to his
Then level them back across the gorge.
All at once
The wedding-night side
Doesn't seem so far.

SUPPLICATION TO SEDONA

Let not your beauty
tempt me to gluttony—
rather, soften
my anticipation—
make me submissive to
the slow and sensual flooding
of your light and shadow,
warmth and rain,
cricket chirp and birdsong,
color—
never sated.

SENTINELS AND SECRETS

Standing in silence
Surrounded by sentinels of stone —
Stirred by their mass,
Stored light and heat,
And centuries of secrets —
I hear them breathe.

Behind a sandstone face,
Inscrutable cum Eliot,
A murmur rises,
"Come in under . . . this red rock,"
Offering succor from the dryness
Of death in life.

Secrets and energy
Poured by the sun
Into these rocks —
Stored
And guarded —
Are trickling into me.

SUMMER DIVIDENDS

Joyfully
we open arms
to family and friends,
who come to share
their time and love—
our summer dividends.

And when they're gone
what bliss it is
to be alone once more
and go to bed
in nakedness
behind an open door.

ON THE DEDICATION OF SEDONA LIBRARY

From every corner of our town,
in demographic sweep,
we came—from young to very old—
with "promises to keep."

Two solid arms of stone reached out
and drew us near the door
of something more than columns,
and roof, and walls, and floor.

A dream come true had called us there.
We came to dedicate
our library—Sedona's jewel—
and also celebrate

Our City's namesake cast in bronze
placed at the entryway.
Sedona was to be unveiled
that crisp October day.

The murmur of the crowd that thronged
our outdoor meeting place
rose like a prayer and seemed to float
above the hallowed space.

And then the Oak Creek Brass struck up;
the speakers spoke their parts—
officials of the library,
the City, and the arts.

Elevating to tradition
a role he'd played before,
beloved Barry Goldwater
cut the ribbon at the door.

In a stirring culmination
that started with a hush,
the sculptor loosed Sedona's drape—
unveiled, she reached to us.

Our hearts reached back, embracing her—
the mayor shared some words—
Sedona's kin were recognized—
the last applause was heard.

These rites, expressing future hopes
born of a common past,
saw separateness exalted to
community, at last!

SEDONA, EARLY MORNING

On early morning walks
mid red rock sentinels,
responding
to gravity
and expanse,
my form elongates—
beyond the summons of shadow—
feet drawn to the earth
and head to the sky
near aerified.

From infinite silence
with acuity beyond myself
I hear callings of birds,
buzzings of a fly,
as from another age
or the distance of another planet.
The sandstone forms surrounding me
breathe out
breathe in
and murmur.

CHRISTMAS DRESSES

Are Christmas dresses still a part
Of every girl child's dreams?
Do their taffetas and velvets
Have memories in the seams?

Somewhere are Christmas dresses
Still hidden underbed
And sewn in secret late at night
With mother-love as thread?

CHRISTMAS ECHOES

In the early hours of Christmas
The warming house expands
Exhaling snaps and pops in the wintry air
That echo childhood years
And colder houses
When I lay in bed with strictured throat
And eyes squeezed tight against the burn
Praying that
Because it's Christmas
Daddy might come home.

HOLIDAY VISITS

One by one
The families come
As answer to my prayer.

From smiling centers
With hugs to last a year.

The days spin by —
I knew they would.
Day/night — day/night — then gone.

But, still, from
Scattered photographs
They reach out — one by one.

FIRST CHRISTMAS WITHOUT THE CHILDREN

I waken early Christmas morn
Aware that we're alone,
Grasping remnants of fleeting dreams —
Of Christmas with children home.

Christmas, when all of us were young —
Those "vision splendid" years
When our arms could circle everyone
And only joy made tears.

And now we graying lovers sleep
Alone in our tinseled house.
No midnight tappings grace our door,
No "Can we get up now?"s.

No pre-dawn bounding from our bed
To stuff the biggest bird —
We'll start our little fowl past noon
And eat with scarce a word.

The rhythm of your breathing breaks.
I sense you're thinking, too,
Of distant loveds — and how this year
There's only me and you.

I turn to your beloved face
And see reflected there —
Midst longing for what used to be —
The joys we yet can share.

We'll build a fire and open gifts —
Make all the Christmas fuss —
Then find the children's Santa mugs
And raise some juice to us.

CLASS REUNION

Under happy-colored canopies
Happy smile meets smile.
Hands reach out to greet —
Remembering.

In mid-festivity
Windswept guys rip from the ground
And lash around us
Forcing recollection of our own uprootings
Our premature partings.
No longer children of the summer
Nor yet fully made
We cling timorously to what unites us
While testing tether to reach beyond.

With darkness, calm descends.
We sit by candlelight
Searching eyes amid the flickers
For reassurance
Reaffirmation.
We speak of those not here
Of those we'll see no more
Then, reaching out, we touch.
Our rites of passage continue.

OF PEPPERMINTS AND HOLLYHOCKS

As in a dream
I trace my steps
Through once-familiar streets
Not aimless
As it seems
But open to remembrance.
The same oppressive sun
That weighed on me in youth
Now comforts me
With strong and shielding arms.

I pass the house where I was born
With stands of hollyhocks
That once were dolls
And parasols
Then walk the street
Where, as a child,
I ran with open lips
To catch the air
And feel it cooling
Past the peppermint
Round and white
I clenched between my teeth.

Oh, yes you can, Thomas Wolfe,
Oh yes you can!

THE HOUSE WAS SOLD TODAY

The house was sold today —
not as the first time,
decades past,
when little boys
and we, so young,
moved on to new adventures —

sold by his mother,
quite matter-of-fact —
we hope with little pain.
His father died here
years ago
and now his mother's gone

to some small room
across the town
where people check her
every hour
and "things"
no longer matter.

The house was sold today —
our first house,
planned to the inch
and saved for
with resolve
to match our dreams.

From empty rooms
that held us close
then served his parents well,
we see through blur of glass and tears
our four o'clock of forty years
still blooms in the window well.

SIREN SONG

What sings to me from some Aegean shore?
—what "something" tempting me through half my days
that bids me now to seek out and explore
the glories that are Greece and bring my praise?

Do her ancient theaters echo yet
the comedies of Aristophanes
and tragedies I will never forget
written by Aeschylus and Sophocles?

What waits for me at Delphi's sacred site?
Athena and Apollo—are they there
with gifts of wisdom, prophecy, and light
in remnants of some oracle or prayer?

What calls to me from Greece's main and isles
in subtle but persistent beckonings?
—what "something" floating through her peristyles—
eternal—wafting on a zephyr's wings?

—the breath exhaled by some Hellenic great?—
Plato, Homer—to be inhaled by me?
O, I shall breathe and feel it permeate
then leave my footprints where theirs used to be!

REMEMBERING THE HIGHLANDS

Succumbing to awe in the highlands—
Near swooning, as under a spell—
I vowed to remember the beauty.
Breathe deep—take it in—mark it well.

My eyes traced a line of circumference,
Sweeping texture and hue inside
The frame that would hold my impressions
Of the high, the deep, and the wide.

A rugged and craggy prominence
Thrust up slate to usurp the scene,
Sundering the Scottish, blue-gray sky—
At the base of its starkness, green.

Not childhood, primary-color green
But green saturated with age—
Historic, tested, confident green—
Of a depth only hearts can gauge.

A lake at the edge of the landscape
Changed from blue to gray—as the sky—
And a dry-stone fence, meandering,
Captivated and drew my eye.

These eyes, nearly blinded by beauty,
Were transfixed in their final sweep—
Scattered as stars in the Milky Way
Were sheep, the ubiquitous sheep.

From harshest bluff to pastoral dell
The foreground pulled it together
With shocks of rugged fragility—
Sweet, purple, remembered heather.

Post Diagnosis

AM I GOING TO DIE?
(Post Diagnosis I)

I do not know about
life after death
but
oh
I know about love
and I don't want to leave you.

OF RADIATION AND CELEBRATION
(Post Diagnosis II)

Never one to squander days
Or wish it were tomorrow
I savor now each second's tick
And every turn of wheel
Along our daily three-hour course
Knowing even radiation
Is cause for celebration
Because we are together.

FINAL FLICKER

There is a final flaring
Before a candle dies —
A surge of light
Extending sight
To weak, unfocused eyes —
Enabling a clearer view
As through a wider door,
Illuminating just beyond
What has been seen before.

My aura flares, diffused and bright;
I burn — my heart beats quicker;
I race in place
Frenetically —
Is this my final flicker?
Oh, Muse, before my fire is quenched
Endow my pen with power
To glorify the commonplace
And celebrate the hour.

GO GENTLE

Hey! This is God's party.
Don't think you have a reservation—
You're only here by invitation,
And was it for the full-fledged bash
Or "cocktails, 6 to 8"?

Mingle with the other guests,
Listen lots, and laugh.
Engage in sparkling conversation
Exploring mankind's situation,
And when it's time for you to leave

Don't overstay your welcome.
Pack up your wit and erudition.
Don't cling. Eschew the admonition
To not "go gentle"—
Then go.

I WILL CELEBRATE THIS DAY

I will celebrate this day—
This day five years ago
I could not know would come,
When I grasped to collect
Every part of my life
For the ultimate cherishing,
Thinking of bargaining
But stopping short
Faced with plenitude.

I will celebrate this day,
Think of five years hence and smile.
I cannot bargain still
But will renew the silent vow
To embrace life's clutter—
The mundane trappings peaked with joy—
Then wrap myself in all its sweetness—
Sunlight, lilacs—
Disclaiming April as "the cruelest month."

I will celebrate this day—
This fraction of the time that's left—
Though it extend my past
And eat into tomorrow.

www.ingramcontent.com/pod-product-compliance
Lightning Source LLC
LaVergne TN
LVHW091231080426
835509LV00009B/1242